Playing with Marbles

Wayan James

Rosen REAL READERS

Rosen Classroom™
New York

Bev and Tim play a game.

They draw a circle.
The marbles go inside.

Bev shoots one marble.

She misses.

Tim aims.

Tim shoots one marble, too.

He hits three marbles.

They roll out of the circle.

Tim wins!

Words to Know

aims

game

marble